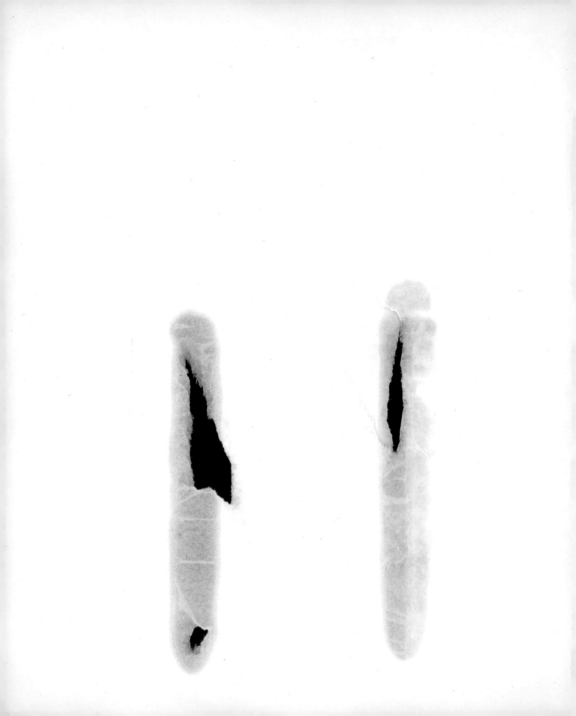

*Water Life*

# Water Life

## JUDITH RODRIGUEZ
*with linocuts by the author*

University of Queensland Press

Also by Judith Rodriguez

*A Question of Ignorance* (in *Four Poets*)
*Nu-Plastik Fanfare Red*

Published by University of Queensland Press, St. Lucia,
Queensland, 1976

Printed and bound by Dai Nippon Printing Co. (HK) Ltd.,
Hong Kong

Designed by Cyrelle

Distributed in the United Kingdom, Europe, the Middle East,
Africa, and the Caribbean by Prentice-Hall International,
International Book Distributors Ltd., 66 Wood Lane End,
Hemel Hempstead, Herts., England.

Acknowledgments: the *Age*, the *Australian, Contempa, Luna,
Makar, Meanjin, Mother, I'm Rooted* (Outback Press), *Nation
Review, New Poetry, Poetry Australia, Poet's Choice 1973,
1974, Quadrant,* the *Saturday Club Book of Poetry, Secon-
dary Teacher, Southerly, Southern Review,* I wish to acknow-
ledge my debt to the Australia Council for the Fellowship I
lived and wrote on in 1974.

— J. R.

*National Library of Australia
Cataloguing-in-publication data*

Rodriguez, Judith, 1936—.
    Water life.

    ISBN 0 7022 1323 3.
    ISBN 0 7022 1322 5 Paperback.

    I. Title.

A821.3

To my Mother and Father

# CONTENTS

## ABOUT THIS WOMAN

**WATER LIFE**

# ABOUT THIS WOMAN

**ABOUT THIS WOMAN:**

green-eyed and could not give them to her children,
caresses her friends in thought, doubts they do likewise,
malingers and charms in fits and starts, dies daily.

About this woman:
wears no ring. Hangs on her husband, hang him,
to be the husband he could be, if he was;
if it takes fifty years. Faithfully mangles him
in words and thought, precarious vindications.

About this woman:
has heard of nymphs like wine; savagely inside
copes with turbid storm-water, and walls of sludge
it piled and can't shift now. The calm nymphs braid
light-runnels, a summer stilled. She dredges
in mixed minds at a quarry-mount of muddle:
where to dump, where gouge, whether
to abandon the site to flood,
worked faces flayed
with rubble in the flurry:

this woman. Tuned to a tangible mode,
score half-composed, corrupt,
exultant, inharmonious, full of trouble . . .

## DOUBLE PORTRAIT

It is the error, the out-of- focus close-up
of the child suddenly running and the child's eye,
hales life, makes sightings

quite apart from the camera's capabilities
and the numbered directions from Kodak, and any refinements
we guess at past that.

With little of Daddy left but a hand, engraved flourish
inclining where she was bound when she changed her mind
and dangling its çoffee-cup,

there survive, as it happens, eyebrows. A kind of tweaked
flotsam, amid the flux of her globe's seething:
the twitch in quicksand.

Her further eye's credible, set in the fleshly horizon.
It disregards pointers, and even when the future snaps!
broods on the bearable instant.

But the unblinked white is ravage, flash-fire, target.
Its eye contracts to irradiated pebble. It signals
the impossible, and reflects nothing,

the landscape salt-scour mostly, shapeless and shadeless.
Light tears up the hairline, scraps surfaces, flattens them burning
against an exposure at speed —

and this that we salvage from the crash is an imitation
of stillness and connections. As a photograph it's wasted,
as a likeness it's bad;

she simply ran in between her dad and a camera.
I keep it to look at, for the whitehot cinder in updraughts
tossing above ash.

Upside down 2nd ed 2/20         11/74

## REBECA IN A MIRROR

Our little tantrum, flushed and misery-hollow,
sits having it out
in a mirror; drawn stiff as it
till her joke of a body, from flat,
flaps with the spasms of crying.
The small eyes frighten
the small eyes clutching
out of such puffed intensity of rage.
She will not look at people about, or follow
a dangled toy. No-one can budge her huge
fury of refusal; being accustomed
to orchards of encouraging faces rolled in her lap,
cloud-bursts of ministering teats and spoons
and the pair of deft pin-welding scavengers
that keep her clean,
she is appalled by her own lonely image.
And we, that she's into
this share of knowledge,
and is ridiculously
comic in her self-feeding anger,
her frantic
blindness by now to the refuge
of a dozen anchoring shoulders and outheld hands,
vassals,
her multitudes . . .

Yet who can be more alone, months walled
in her cot's white straw,
the family hushed
and hovering, afraid to touch
so small
a trigger of uproar;
or so much as flutter
one of her million or more
petulant rufflers spoiling for noise and action
around the nerve-end flares that signal ruction?

6

And think, she has not long come
through a year of twilight time in one gradual place
further and faster
than death, or the endless relays
of causeless disaster;
frail-cauled, a hero, past perils vaster than space
she has come —
and can never re-enter
the unasked bodily friendship
of her first home.

## THE RUGS

The children are growing out
of me, wider than trees or rooms —
all four something of both,
each more than both together.
Of trees and rooms to write
is easier done than not,
but rhyming to or about
children, for me their mother,
lies inconceivably far
in dissembling self-regard
from their live birth-beds.

Exact Ben Jonson sadly
knew his young children dead
fit then for tenderest words.
            I accordingly
fiddle and knot, working
whole hives of hexagons
stored with the juice of summer
for rugs for children's beds,
and stitch in the seasons' emblems
rather than trust to poems
written or said.

## THE SCISSORS

Taken with the others, she's the alien;
you adore her, star-faced tyrant, or abhor.
She is paying me out for my dark tutoring of her —
tries scissors on her arm to test our bargain,
looks me in the eye. I see myself
older than her, with nail-scissors, waiting for blood
to dot in fat little holes on my wrist, done alone
for the scar and interest. Like this too, for a dare:
Stop me, God. Try to. (Can you abuse too far?)
She has taken me aback, across, to knowing more
about daughtering, about the connection, prefiguring her
delighted firework. Even when I copy my mother's
cold water way with hysterics, I celebrate Mine
from her foghorn voice to her turn-in fling of the left foot,
from her arch affectionate gusts to her positive blood,
apt hand and greedy eye-play. Brown to my green.

The pole 1                                          22'74

## POLAR

As near as dammit to midday
and out of a clear sky;
the casual approach had me in there,
craning to keep with
the tall girl in a pink gingham
skirt sauntering
south to my 50 — 40 —35
north on Wai-ora,
the easing back exactly sufficient
to keep her covered, all
but a heel, swung hair and the air of smugness
about a telegraph pole;
which is a pretty good reason to dig
poles up and burn them, only
that was all that caught my natural adoration
in a half-hour drive, so
till I hit a pole, following pink gingham
at the corner of my eye,
maybe it's as good a reason as any
for keeping them.

## RAPUNZEL IN MIDDLE-RISE

She suns above the junction.
A twelve-year-old dreamed her, the time
of tutelary witches;
hair you could sit on, and a tower
to sit on it in.
She is flying a tress for lovers
and won't come down.

Half-glazed, five floors from traffic,
her niche commands us;
just what the old women offered.
She can dry her hair in the updraught
and outwait a change of keepers,
knowing the tradition of happiness
by inalienable descent.

And we, lined up at the lights,
spot her, and squint through thickset
signals, ads, wires.
Regulations keep passing us on
Regulations keep passing us on
like litter and public holidays;
red signs have the walkers guessing;

she is all the brambles in sight.
For her, air opens vortices —
the swinging in parks, steering cars,
or turning in to a four-day bender
at the corner pub. Circulation
is the one step forward she is dying for:
to go shares in a million lives!

The newspaper twitches behind her
on the wiped kitchen table
as the million reach out.

## 5AM REDBRICK

After the night's
                unbeautiful tears
smeared and unshared,

                being awake and walking
mazes of corners
                in the high half-lit room
slippers a-drag
                in the lumpiness of second-hand carpet
and misshapen underfelt,

                after a time of staring
at humped silence
                and sagged oversewn seams'
wry rucking:

                The wide windows are washed,
                the sky is a Mediterranean
                pale vista full suddenly
                of light and fine wind . . .
                down the street, paired housefronts
                of upright redbrick wade
                from gardens of shadow, hailing
                sky; they open their hearts
                earth-red and warm as toast.
                And burn to closed curtains.

## DESERTING

Weathering fire: the parade and figment
of a woman who has left a home
speaks politely in corridors with her husband
and makes time for the children's sports-days.

The fire-front's ragged and will hardly flare.
It is all along the ridge
but she scored a break this side. It will be contained.
Still yes it plays, yes it flicks

if ever her smile-lines, if ever her eyes
let up, and her stance and her hands
vary from their schedule of energized total living.
She is on, she is off, the white-heart coal,

festive, it is rollicking, this freedom, it is
high-handed, tight-lipped, livewire,
strung up to be capable, to attend, yet such inconsequent
timbres and pause blur and jag

her endured directionless monotone; gustily
the burnt-out tract smoulders,
whole light-years are kittenish at her ruffles, the hands writhe,
words whiten. We look on, and are let off.

## A LONG WAY FROM MISSISSIPPI

Too lightly, like candour
she steps her scrunched toes in dirty sandals
through states of regular yankees;

a stir to crease
the compliant chamois, her flesh-
admitting dress

resurgent
against commonplaces of union.
Half-furled, proud as bourbon

she is making no sense today,
goes without fuss to a different table
(plotted trajectory of the free agent)

and reminisces;
routs Grant, flouts schoolbook history.
"*We* only stood to sing Dixie."

Night window-piece 2/20                                    '74

## MEETING APART

This was the way they met:
one by the bay and one
by the stone-set railings.

They had spoken of time and place:
the flat, after nine. Both sat
till late, silent

in their separate cars and lives —
with waves coming dark, and the lanes
alongside North Carlton's

burying-ground, darker
and dead still. Till counting the crests
breaking, the sounds

of couples slowing down
into shadows, or home, each rallied
the grounds for going.

**SCENE:**

I come into the room, talking,
switch on the light, go to the window, stand straight
looking from cell to sunlight:

See, the four-stride verandah
and the docile iron curled round the purposes of men
and this high room, mine, with its eye

to the chance of words, footsteps,
snippets of sky and subjects of the corridor.
You come into the room, talking.

I lie down, put my feet up straight
on their ridiculous ply bed-head. Life pools quietly
in the walls. I am still, I forbear,

you lean down, you kiss my face,
my eyes fill with tears, skies. I close them.
You come into the room, talking.

## CHARM: TO RECEIVE A LETTER

Anxiously owed a letter, balancing
good news and bad — the let-down, the lift,
the jolt, and the stringing-along —
trust it to come
for months

but don't write. Remember, you couldn't care less.
You tot up dates, guess at news, not attending
to the never-of-course-to-be-shaken
message-wagged grapevine;
maintain

the martyr's air, aware of merit but humble.
Ripen reproaches, clutch — dig them under;
write, tear it up. Such fits
churn the grudge thick,
make it stick.

Finally, patience to tatters, past assuming
causes out of varieties of human
breakdown, hiatus, crisis,
whatever — throw pride in
by writing,

straining back rancour. Send. The letter-box
offers straightway the word your opposite
wrote, to the hour, on the spell's end.
(At expense of baring
your caring.)

## UNSENT LETTER, WITH DOODLE

May I catechize you? *no you cannot say no*
*at a letter's distance* DRAWING THE HORNS OF A RAM
LIKE QUERIES REVERSED *and meant as statement not question*
*I am catechizing you* One  IT IS A VERY TAME
ALTOGETHER PACIFICALLY ORIENTED CEREMONIOUS RAM
OF A GOAT OF A GOD MERE MUTTON IS OUT OF THE QUESTION
You do not write to me *talk to me my existence thins*
*the reverberations are bad no ask Aren't you writing*
*to me any more* THE GOAT TURNS *I don't hear the answer*
HIS CRAZED GOLD SLIVER OF EYE FLICKERS I FALL
TO DESIGNING HIS GAMBOLS *but no more questions.*

## ON MARRIAGE

I appeal to the fabulous loves
and their rare, futile occasions
all the time, every time
we remain, etc.,
financially, especially, MARRIED:

kindly as kitchen knives, unmatched,
dull, rubbed lank as habit . . .
Catullus, blessed with disdain
and acrimony, how am I to rhyme
this contemptible collusion?

Rill St. permutations A 2                                    21/74

## LYING LATE SUNDAY MORNING

*for Fabio*

Encapsuled in morning sloth, our daughters gone
at their chancy trot down the passage, to clamber for apples
over toybox and bookshelf, and wind up the world of noise;
propped on our blanketed strand, the brass bed clear
of a junkheap of shoes and overblown gardens of hankies
and socks and a dead-dog stool, we are left to graze
fatness of age and sun.

Look! at the top of our rising field of tiles
taking off east, black as print, there stand at tactics
magpies, you might say, knowing no second word.
Two of them fit to release from a hand, but the big fellow
a lump like a bucket, a beak to terrorize backblocks
decades of Goldilocks gleaming to school, with his lurch
and his sawmill shriek and his spiking

beating down out of windbreak pines. But this raider
has mislaid his joystick. It glints in the anyhow mess
of his nest, forgotten, while he glowers and ruffles and hunches,
tail-feathers half-mast. We quell our fears for the quizzical
pair with this goose-heavy lout; then amazed, see one rise,
rocket over, and sputter and stab till the monster launches
sullenly, spitfires at his head.

Well! if that's kindly Nature's morning mood,
give us four whited walls and the floor's disarray.
Or less. Or even more . . . I retreat, I fulfil the enclosure
of your shoulder where I fit, and lie along your side
and from the close order of us see nothing awry,
only how spirited sheets mimic our pleasure
and everything is renewed;

how through the fall and shine of motes, wall
flickers, a little shoal of light-panes swim,
contract to regular chips, then disappear.
On the steady drawer-fronts sun-flecks circle in consort,
their laces of light plucked in time to a mirror's
earth-paced turning; the gilt ray glides on air,
jewels leap in grain, brass flowers; it all

showers from a column of silver facets, a showy
vase of the 1930's rimmed and based
with chrome worn thin by my childhood eye of devotion,
its laundry years, and the puzzled regard of this room
for my stiff-necked indulgence of sentimental taste;
how the dazzles zoom to a course of children's commotion
returning: a Rebeca, a Zoë!

## FLOWER-POEM

After the straight talking-to
after the whining and sulks
after the touch of the rope
after the sneers of defiance
after being lectured and raged at

for sneaky scufflings with his sister
and taunting to tears 'little hosts'
and barbarous bumping through the entire
showing of their Daddy's film;
after school-ground dogfights and dudgeon;

he offers, sort of careless,
his by-the-way branch-spoils
committed to a missile of a school-bag
and retrieved now, black-fingered, panting;
two wattle-sprigs, two not;

chooses the goldy mug
and sets it all up, still telling
aloud the leaves' difference;
centres it to a large table-top
and flings off to fresh havoc.

## AT THE NATURE-STRIP

In Lantana Street's mid-morning
an Italian grandmother is trying to happen.

The nature-strip's flat out parching.
All the hardy natives in sight have leaves on;

the garbos were through before the kids went,
the Council street-cleaner's rotary whiskers

slurped by at 6.30. All day begonias
are for nobody, till early each evening hoses them.

Mrs. Whatwasitagain in black
is gazing cobbles out of half-melted bitumen,

also whitewash from her hillside village;
and nudging one-language housefronts into gossip

to boast of her Mimo, the smart one,
and of big Vito, tossing pizze downtown,

and Nino, in Bari, who'll be out soon.
Till a carload of shoulders cruising past

bare-faced and noisy as tourists
stalls under her arms-across watching,

worn shoe-heels planted,
head-scarf, and the front-on placid wrinkles;

they pick up in low — leave her standing —
half-focused — an exotic — too old, and simply

out of place. (Whose roots settle
for earth, old earth, with a blackboy endurance.)

# FINISHING A FILM AT THE GARDENS

Up out of shadow
    from the concert bowl's
bat-slung day-sleeping cavern
    came climbing
onto Sunday's echoless slopes
    our stranger,

    that flying morning
where tangled in focus and shutter
    I ranged
assorted flappable daughters
    in duffel coats
    for late clear autumn

with Conte's bronze woman
    perched on her tripod,
    intent
    on the concert of air
and wearing round her the shining
    city;

the American with young-grey hair
    live face
and no need to explain
waved me into the frame
    and took,
    the last of the roll.

It turns out the shutter was stuck
    and the group came to nothing.
    He went off
    nameless,
    his gift a blank.
All the same, a picture worth having.

## OCCASION FOR ELEGY

That was your gibe: I was waiting
for people I knew to die
so as to agonize elegies
and monkey with memory;

but that was when I was younger.
Now I'm near forty, I'm wary
of the body all booby-traps
and the world-wide cemetery,

reminiscence slippery as rot
and loyalty much like libel,
compassion that gobbles down horrors
and suffering worse than I feel.

Most of the dead I can let be.
Rememberers need not raise
and refurbish each part-grimed image
with draperies of phrase.

I grow simpler, I yearn for what's young,
not the death-keyed negative
but light on leaf, and children
that never mean not to live.

Backyard 10/20　　　— For David Malouf　　　4/75

## 10,000 ACCUSERS

All the hundred hundred poems
    that I didn't have the wit,
energy or devotion to commit!

I glimpsed their shapes, and jotted down
    reminders or a phrase.
They reproach me later, hanging round for days

but rarely close for long enough
    forr me to learn their ways.
Somewhere they wait unborn, for men more fit

to meet and recognize them
    and retrieve them from their unlit
place, and dress them humanly, and raise

them up voices. Hearing them mingle
    notes that I could not hit
is joys under accusation, it betrays

the casual, covetous heart
    which yet finds grace to praise
the fostering into song of each tentative spirit.

## SPIDERS

### Spider-move

Ready as rain's

precipitous
pause
in the course of
pane or leaf,

and gathering amid
shins
his pattern of unfriend,
the web-

still

SPIDER

suddenly

quick
as a scatter of tacks
fillip
of hay on wind

scuttled over
petals stone
bark glass
gloss finish . . .

gone.

**Conducting spider**

Reared on his stagey dark-barred
spread, has notation by heart,

reads merely my ruthless stance
wielding a shoe to flatten him,

bunches in his corner, rapt,
then travels his deftly-orchestrated

set of variations with cadenza.
Elegant, this keeping on waving,

but his run's fluent as bushfire;
looking's a touch less futile

than burnishing the paint or chrome
of his way home, to murder a cadence.

**Meditation of spider**

I am rebuked alike for my shrinkings at spider
and my Let that end him.
None rebukes spider
than unannounced by night he besets my spaces.

We are within my walls. But upon his ground.
I flurry to the tug of his silks.

How to be at one with this swinger, clambering, retracing,
that reels out around him endless himself?
How to reckon the dense press of his artisan urge,
loft to his lyric top-trace?

What weaver woven, leads here his bellying weft?
and spreads, fisherman, his network of live
self for a seive to air, walks sure
his equation of dance, snare, scavenger.

His meditation of spider.

Is he predator, that for his prey plots
constellations by morning?
Artist, to devour his following?
I am broken on the spokes of spider's dark competence.

## AFTER A POETRY SEMINAR

Litter of white foolscap:
stepping-stones
for prey, for huntsmen.
Our echoes range across reams

slowing, musing, in doubt
constrained to dangle
opaquely after
sudden forms, live sunlight.

Beside the traces, read . . .
some nervous creature
stands hardly breathing
at the heart of this tangle we thread

in a mood of trespass, and hunters
before us have printed
the morass. Scents mix.
Whose then is the track we're running

to its last red dint on the river-bank?
Whose wound, whose burden
gives place here to words
sideways their black weight moving?

## THE QUESTIONER IN BLACK

All the years of her life
she has braved the skull

All the centuries of her civilization
she has embraced the skull

All the pores of her flesh
she has taunted the skull

Every line of her verse
looks out from the eye-sockets

At the end of the writers' dinner
she rehearses the rising

of black windy song
in the missing throat:

I am still young — nearly,
I write, I am alone,

how shall I live?
how shall I live?

## A LIFETIME DEVOTED TO LITERATURE

In your twenties you knew with elegiac certainty
you would die young. Your father's heart attack
tallied, a verification.

Thirty was your worst year: the thirties fatal to genius,
and genius undeclared by the would-be oracles.
You gave thought to publication;

then a news item — friend dropped dead in the street —
co-eval, a get-up-and-go editorial
viceroy at thirty-four —

cheered you somehow. You planned aloud and in detail,
publishers ventured for you, reviews came your way
as you learned to joke and your hair thinned,

and several thromboses onward you inhabit unruffled
an active advisory presence: a sitter on Boards
preparing to live for ever.

Buses pass here daily 4/20

174

## IN THE VANGUARD

His name I heard rumour'd — the revolutionary poet.
Restor'd to these circles a year now — yet I had not encounter'd him —
from the stateside visit. I enquir'd of the host, I view'd him,
trim headband, beard hearty, slab of red-shirted back,
unmodulated robustness; a being declaim'd here;
did his poems come thick-stamp'd, fist-raising manifestoes?
Of his reading I remember how we still'd, leaning forward; how the hand —
the hand that had written, his tense and fluttering right hand —
gently, constrictedly, from the 3rd to the 4th shirt-button
tripp'd, conducting the inner affectionate harmonies
of a wholly conventional, wistfully sensitive poem.

## GURU SESSION

The house is sacred to the arts, the company invited.
The poet shows up, a plain white kaftan,
and is very quiet inside it,

garlanded simply at the neck with leaves and tendrils
and a shading of beard, with acknowledgments to blue-green
nature, and small sequins.

His profile's gilded, the shaded lamp poised
so; an armchair receives him, cross-legged on velvet.
The typescript glimmers, turning . . .

Few passions, we know, can be crowned with memorable poems.
It is given to few bare feet to be anything but ugly.
This of his, sandalled,

achieves recollection: the arrowy downward middle toe
barbed with converging others — unrehearsed, I take it,
the enactment of a foot of talent.

## REPORT TO THE ANTHROPOLOGY CENTER

Another thing we observed, among the mild
and nervous men and women of this race:
often at the clearing, one would leave a place
in the daily line-up for questioning (hereafter styled
*conference*); and stroll back later on. Quite wild;
our guess is — woodland's made them shy of space.
And many, both women and men, answered with face
null, and no reasons — all the while carrying some child
or holding it close. It's possible they gained
security by it, something to hold on to
(probably basically visceral? in their drained
vegetarian way). Where the absentees had gone to,
how the tribal psyche's conditioned on a perch —
these topics need more resources for research.

## HOW COME THE TRUCK-LOADS?

Somehow the tutorial takes an unplanned direction:
anti-Semitism.
A scholastic devil advances the suggestion
that two sides can be found to every question:

Right.
Now, who's an anti-Semite?
One hand.
Late thirties, in the 1960's. Bland.
Let's see now; tell us, on what texts or Jews
do you base your views?
There was a landlord, from Poland, that I had.
Bad?
A shrug. Well, what did he do?
Pretty mean chasing up rent. Ah. Tough.
And who
else? No-one else. One's enough.

The mill-stone (Juniper Tree) 7/20                    16/75

## CHILE 1973

Jara, your grey-nailed hands
play a mean guitar.

They were men of feeling, yes,
who set the hands free:

could not bring themselves
to tear out the tongue!

saw how you'd sing — Jara
and his dead arms!

Clearly, they'd made a mistake.
Something had to be done.

Victor Jara, you don't need hands now
to die in the stadium.

Hands, here are men to play,
a million arms for you.

How do the hands go, Pinochet?
Do you sleep to the tune?

## DETAIL FROM A MIDWINTERLEARLECTURE

And if towards world's end
the age-old patterns
of pebble, petal, shell
all failed,
and the too-faithful snail
left off his tracking
ways in our garden bed;
with any time on our hands
habit would settle
for making friends
of tiny shapes of metal;

or so it appeared,
with the lecturer clearing round
Lear's gilded fly
perspectives of scholarship.
His left forefinger flashed
on a rung of flesh
the pet he'd found
and pinned there
to wear and fiddle with:
the tight-clinging, upright, spry
silvery paper-clip.

## DIVINATION

The mind's palm unclenched
tilts for deciphering
chance-found palpable sherds:

black-banded lip of a jar,
line and loop outside;
and the lighter chip striped with brown.

I put them down, shut them away
with a broken die
and a yellowing knuckle-bone.

They did for their day that's gone
and leave to divine
the screw that augered the thread

in steel, and the shape a curve
of clay defines,
and the mortal limb and the mind.

## PACHELBEL'S CANON

To have dreamed first the notes  
                   of the unassailable round  
then with ample gesture first  
                   describe its octagonal precinct,  
the five men intent  
                   in their room's unfolding resonance;  
to press the beat on the 'cello  
                   with grave perfected passion  
or clang alongside unhasting  
                   chords of a courtly insistence;  
to lead the trace of sound,  
                   pass it back, pass on from it, weavingly  
take up the trace, pass it back,  
                   pass on taking up — generations —  
tread the steps of three dancers  
                   that shadow the eight trees' circle  
(time and the figure recrossing  
                   dividing the constant ground)  
O and spiral, poise, and quiver  
                   in the changes, dressed wood flowering;  
then bear into gliding measure  
                   of long boughs and grass in wind-welter —  
all that least understands  
                   finality at caesura:  
to be still, ear blessed in the cadence,  
                   soul awakened to order.

The broken pane 4/20

174

*— For Ian Rasmussen*

## I CALL CHILDREN TO SEARCH GRASS

I call children to search grass, I marvel that days hold
pine-trees of great-poled wide-rigged elegance
root-striding our hill, cone-scattering in season.
How barely they in the midst of limitation lean,
weathering above sorties vowels longer than these generations!

## TOWARDS FOG

The quality of fog is that it has style but no detail.
Though detected in a state of nuance, it cannot be caught at it.
I try with a 2B — softly — with a 6 or 8B — I am gradual as growing —
still there are lines, parts, separations. Fog has none.
When was a photograph of fog, a film of fog moving,
ever so diffuse, directionless, and all-round-clammy?
And the incuriosity of fog is beyond everything.

There are times I want to go back to somewhere like beginning.
The concept of a cell is too advanced for what I want to be, sometimes.
Words are cellular, and baulk at it: fog is not-saying.
Fog engulfs. Devours, with no process. Fog is instead of.
Fog extends. Fog bulks. It is nothing you ever see in profile, yet there . . .

What is *there*? I put out my hand. Is that a handful of fog?

Does it flow through? And can I expel it with a willed clenching?
Or invite it with nebulous fingers, tendons in concert — the hand half-opening?

Mind revving up to understand, body boggling
at the falling to inorganic, the going nerveless;
both fall short, bailed up on recognized borders.
The true photograph of fog would disappear,
its corners sucked into monochrome lack of point.
And the drawing of fog would be made with
horizonless sky and land for a pencil.
And the poem of fog would fold
round the wire-thin word *today-as-usual*
all the sounds, ideas of all kinds of being
in a more than pastoral silence.

The man as fog does not bear thinking of.
Green though the slopes are, after.

49

I displace fog, yet it is inward with me.
I can't do fog. Never, perhaps, to be done with it —
exhalations from a deep place, earth-rumours
fragile and huge, a beauty of a threat
there's no dealing with.

# WATER LIFE

## RUDIMENTARY LANDSCAPE

Where banks, grey-grassed,
greening along the rim,
round in their obdurate cast
grey mud, sad water,
we look across between
our sullen bridges of concrete
that murmur on concrete props.
Opposite, an earth-heap juts;

marooned there, fifty round
grey sand-smooth stones
await placing, each
humbly itself and its kind.
They're not arranged or piled,
just there. No human settling
unmysteriously arrives
at such bare random location;

till, unaware of spectators,
the bunched hummock slings
to the sky, wheeling, its stones
that skitter wide and hang
glinting, then round the gums:
things break to a sketch of spirit.
Eyes waken. We trail the gulls
as the dull bank takes wing.

## RECONNAISSANCE

There, circling the lone
river-flat heaped with clean fill —
mounds rough as tipped
but laced with flowering weed:
the water-bird.

Crawling wide, hush the engine.
Mess or no mess
he picks a way in, unfussed,
grey, private, fastidious.
White-ringed, the eye

stares over hummocks, atop
poisings and levellings of his neck.
Towards a nest, perhaps,
his spindle legs course
dead tangles

on the dumped muddled loads
and obstinate chance-set growing things.
His black nib startles to a pause —
adjusts  to slant lower —
dots and adds;

then suddenly he's off into wilderness,
seen across brown fern
gadding, urbanely curious
in the city of his desolation.
And is gone.
                    I move on.

**BACKING OUT**

Upside-down greyness: the scrubby gums
worry and backtrack in water moving across
that still goes on spreading. Such watery morning
cloud in sunlight, such ruffled willow-lined levels
among their hummocky shores, but will not quite shimmer;

this is the stretch where the heron rambles on clay
and over tussocks; the bushes have him considering.
For a whole short age of lagoon-time we can't pick him
till his cry grates, he's up, and his emblemed wings foldingly
lift and spurn and lift from the line of flight.

Out from behind the car-door where bending and peering
they followed his finicky stroll, the children run
for his rising away; and are stopped in the gluepot mud
of the unmade road bulldozed for human going
he touched on, just printing. The shoes will take hours to clean.

## CHANGING THE SUBJECT

I thought I had come to see the car,
a sports, all its get-up-and-go
line and shine
gone —
the gesturing bars
that held a windscreen once, incredibly
bulldozing air,
rusted past rescue —
too abject now, even without sun,
for wings to perch upon.

As I came turning down from the road
bumping from rut to ridge
all burred with gravel
to the flat
(maybe the way they dragged it in)
the sports disappeared.
There among dirt skid-marks a green-headed parrot
sidled and skittered in wind
off towards red-hot pokers by the water
I shouldn't wonder.
I discovered that that
was what I had come to find:
the thing that mattered,
jarring
and imperious as orange and green,
that ran off apart in the grass, took its downright way without waiting
and commanded the looking at.

## BOYS, ROPE, GUM-TREE

There were these two boys, at nine,
setting their rope in half-sunshine.

They'd thrown it on the biggest gum's
great branch; one swarmed, his mate swung

by the paddock grey with wet.
They went to it, in their grey sweaters,

customary and secret as the man
every day on the shelved bank yabbying

across the lagoon; spoke little,
made backs and clambered, rose clinging into

a world of tree time.
Meaning to hitch the rope higher,

what boy wouldn't lie and trace
paths in the sombre weed, acres

of mornings and afternoons;
or was it some knot of the tree's roomy

hand that held him? and the other
at rope's end, face up, not a word uttered,

following from where he stood?
How should the hours strike, school-boys

passing along the ridge
call them, a bell ring? See, stillness

recoils, they are down and snatch
their bags from the half-dry slope, scramble

for the fence at the top, and run.
The mist is off the lagoon, sunlight

shrivels gum-leaves to tin
and greys to a standstill the rope left swinging.

## GIGGLE HEARD AMONG GUM-TREES

Get that, a fantastic miniature
wiggle it goes and trips
weightless and prettily
unselfconscious as linked
coins at ears, a gilt-tasselled ring.

The large air contemptuously does not need
to receive it:

properly, it spills in a hollow
among details of pebble and fern
and follows down
capillary evasions of the stream.
Trees close in, elaborating
tricks in the tendril thread
of its restless working,
the never-quite-excited
flicker of an oscillograph.

Little things trace it almost out of ken —
clicks in the underbrush, a sigh,
a dry leaf clenching,
the seepage failing.
And always there is lichen,
somewhere, scribbles on;

a patch of blue kicks out the middle branches
and loud from lower down
where falls quarry the scarp
up, vaulting rock-faces, starts
the laugh, the laugh.

## AT THE MEETING OF WATERS

Down where the gullies meet
the fallen gum-tree rides
at the world's centre.

It is up from the grass that claims it,
down from its hold on sky.
Alive with its death.

I ride there to be alone,
said the girl, where the gullies meet
in among the hills,

and water coming away off the land
never staying, runs to creeks,
river-levels, sea-levels;

the lapse of root, soil, rock
gnawing the years grown round
in this earth-held wood.

And where gullies meet, and the tree
sucks on its breast of sky
and goes to ground,

the taste of its white silence
the taste of its red core
in the air, in the earth,

are translated in words of water:
*I embrace, I embrace*, to my furthest
salt reaches raked with wind.

The floating stick "4/20                    47/75

## AMBIENCE

Moving over her glass-fluent body
found fingers tendril-tipped
a viny profusion
tonguing sea-shapes and salt wind
the rash skin quick as a wound's
always feeling
moving  over her glass-fluent body;

living amid her seasons' shifting
currents and tidal variations
fed oarsmen to breakers
purged distinctions of love
parted wrack, roused angels
moving over her glass-fluent body's
oceanic persistence.

## JELLYFISH

In languor afloat
I lean, *medusa*,
   on the tides' trail.

And need not waken.
Frontless and faceless
my allargando's
slow going closes
in confrontation:
I countenance all
comers, with pursed mouth,
the not-to-be-prised,
the clenched-on-pulsing,
the veiled-and-behung-
with-eddying-frayed-
fringes-of-tassels
immutable valve;

     I mouthe.
I winnow oceans;
I fill them. Floating

## BIVALVE

Conforming right now to the norms
neither of courtship nor teaching
the open side of my face spreads out
the closed side tightens.

If this goes on
my head will be a clam slewed sideways
in all the stew of my sea-bed spaces
and will never sit straight on
such the push and wash of its element.

If you try to get round it
you will only be taken in
by the bland loom of liquid expansions.
On the other tack
there's no open approach to the simple
hinge built round with rock
precisely

and I do not despise it;

the wide side of me there with its undulant plush
expanding exploring incessantly
and its nerve-ends softer than water
shrieking on grit and ululating at ease
is there to supply the fit
of my unprised grip
my quick and holding bit.

One side the drying knot.
The other
the pulsing mass shimmers
to farm its parasite
and silkenly tugs my focal creature tight
in his grotto of blood
to usages of light.

64

Self-portrait 5/20                    5'74

## MANATEE

Just the same, the poem of the manatee
will not go away. It keeps inshore,
keeps disappearing in the tale
of sightings, encounters, caresses;
massive habitue, mortally
ready to be flesh, of the lull
and shallows of your Floridan sea-board.

There, daylight balances
in a cup, the manatee imperturbably
forages the river-mouth. Sweet passes
to salt, the measure of sun
and distance to the skim of water,
weed loses count and clouds
the pools, straggling herds-wide;

whose people, sinking slowly
to pasture, improbable as Zeppelins,
have never been told what happened
to Steller's sea-cow, two centuries
and an ocean away. Nor asked, what
survives here? Things that lie still,
things that have cover, the armour-clads,

what man lets be. This surely, this
interval, no-man's-land, weed-crammed
sand-bottoms, weed-streams, weed-seasons
and the calm exemplary nation
of lump-faced eaters of weed
browsing, suckling, circling
weedways of visionary twilight.

Poem, boulders that drift,
submarine idyll, silences
incomprehensibly large!

Here come the divers, bubbling
their little quick land-words, working
the frog-feet they learned to reach you,
juggling weed-trails and historic emotions;

they goggle — the mermaid bears
into focus. The death of sailormen's
an undesigning body, after all:
huge-pored, hare-lipped and bald,
the stare one weed-thought, the hide
an aged impervious tolerance
of weed, hide, hands . . .

What did they see in her, those press-ganged
years of pemmican and the lash?
Fresh meat in parting foam —
good men jumped in and the wake
unrolled to tent their feast;
man-eater for sure. The creature's
researched now, re-conceived,

civilized and cast in a cattle-part
for our old crepuscular dream
of man and the peaceable monsters.
Only, men hardly learn
undersea purposes, and course
circuits of deluded will
dandling the enigma; to end

with utility, Midlands farmers
in a Stubbs, dwarfed by their stud
uncaring bulls. The manatee
ignore curious glass,
move against the little limbs
assured of their region, torpidly
hand-feed, and never think to bite.

## POEMS DROWNING

Every day they drown in dozens
clawed down, or land throttled
trailing the venemous deadlines.
They clog my cracks
they die by inches
day rises and quivers
and rises and is unaware.
In the end there is nothing left of them.

But you, poem,
sighted so close to surfacing,
you I will have out
if it's by the hair;
yes this one, alive
or nearly —
by assault or guile
by the feet or the hair
or anything handy or even halfway fair.

## POEMS FISHED OUT

Midnights
I sit in the bath
writing;
dead upright
(you'd laugh)
unseeing and quite asleep.

Poem drafts
and sketches go
slapping down into the drink;
I come to

and have them all out in no time,
childhood ink bleeding.
Blood's better off
— it clots —
and jottings in biro;
but old heartfelt inks
flush and merge
to the touch of sea. Nightly
I dab with towels
at ink-stains, flood-blotches,
the remains of washed-out words,
identify
and encourage survivors
gathering their draggled crowds
— laying out sheets to dry.

Woman creating ⁹⁄₂₀                                    19/75

**ESKIMO OCCASION**

I am in my Eskimo-hunting-song mood,
Aha!
The lawn is tundra     the car will not start
the sunlight is an avalanche     we are avalanche-struck at our breakfast
struck with sunlight through glass     me and my spoonfed daughters
out of this world in our kitchen.

I will sing the song of my daughter-hunting,
Oho!
The waves lay down     the ice grew strong
I sang the song     of dark water under ice
the song of winter fishing     the magic for seal rising
among the ancestor-masks.

I waited by water to dream new spirits,
Hoo!
The water spoke     the ice shouted
the sea opened     the sun made young shadows
they breathed my breathing     I took them from deep water
I brought them fur-warmed home.

I am dancing the years of the two great hunts,
Ya-hay!
It was I who waited     cold in the wind-break
I stamp like the bear     I call like the wind of the thaw
I leap like the sea spring-running.     My sunstruck daughters splutter
and chuckle and bang their spoons:

Mummy is singing at breakfast and dancing!
So big!

## WATER A THOUSAND FEET DEEP

I stand washing up, the others have gone out walking.
Being at the best, I am homing in on the worst:

to choke in indifferent waves, over ears in ocean —
skim of earth's sweat — what immensities of salt fear
drench us and tighten — with children to save or lose,
the choice, as from old gods, which to consign to destruction:
how to riddle out waste and defiance? what line cast?
what crying hope hold to? for there is no deciding,
it acts itself, the damning sequence secret
as origin and universe, life as an improvisation
on terrors . . .

the tearaway undertow. But I never lose grasp on my son
or stop swilling plates and setting them to drain;

till blatantly the door. The boy ran ahead of the rest
and is home. I let him in panting, he trails me insisting
Hey, Mum, so close, there is so much floating known here
between us, have we trod the same waters? Hey, Mum,
is there water a thousand feet deep? Yes, I say,
emptying the sink, and give him figures, the soundings
of ocean trenches, which are after all within measure.
As if in the context of fathoms he'd made a mistake
and it mattered.

Family 6/20

31/174

## LATE MEETING, LARGS

but boy's activity and child's toy
become a sombre ritual of praise
to God . . .        — *Largs Bay*, by Donald Maynard


Reading road-maps, reading Mozart, reading
your poem that I don't have with me
reading your heart

offering the marvel of joy, offering this morning
to memory and the day-filled distance
fifteen years after

our eyes made landfall, met upon words half-happy,
strained against difference and drift,
embraced in departing;

I have come to Largs.


Keeping track. Keeping faith, keepsakes; never quite on purpose
keeping a little saucer you left me
when you cleared your flat

and went away south. It had never been simple seeing you
and never would be, no sun
rounding us in

but a vigil of cities, contrivance, encounters and countering.
Nothing of yours to brim
a white saucer's round

till I face from the land

Largs Bay to northward, its ages of ocean wind
laid in midday calm.
Things farc solitary,

beach-wall of rocks, kiosk, pier, a signal-tower
for the Outer Port, at the rim
where coast nudges sky;

and right here, wide walkable beach and a few odd shells.
I pair two, enclose a pebble —
all ill-matched

as acts of sentiment


to making out lives past. Making them up more likely,
or worse, only making sense.
Back at the car

the pulse engages a schedule; reverse, St. Joseph's,
your nun and your boy playing ball
a poem's summer . . .

Our winter flare-up, I could make nothing of you
but orphaned yearnings — my own.
I could barely sketch them

but you told me, keep drawing;


and see, meeting here, we round the shore-line's single
perspective in the doublings of time.
That day you praised

praise in a sunlit leaping at play, is mine
to lead remembrance travelled
to the make of a poem

and rejoice in our breaking together and drawing apart;
as sand-shapes and sea under wind
beat and wait,

meet to endless remaking.

## PENELOPE AT SPARTA

So this is Helen. I used, she says, to be
so fine — such skin, such a waist, a really tiny waist!
her blue eyes looping through wine. She surfaces bewildered,
her fingers flap their exclaimings — she is half-seas over.
And my belly — I was beautiful; my belly, it was white, smooth, tight.
Just one baby it took to spoil it, you can't imagine.

She needs no Troy. Simple-stepping Menelaus
has the boys a-shout on the back slope and keeps filling glasses.
All she requires is a hearing. Odysseus, she says, Odysseus,
your wife s very clever  very definite. You're a lucky man.
She understands you; anybody can see it.
And I too, going downhill I've discovered I have something to offer;
with people, just humanly, I've talents; they say I'm quite managing.
I've always known you had depths, impossible to get at,
now you must tell me. You must sit here, on the floor,
come on, I can see it suits you.

Menelaus and I are well-trained, we have that in common.
I sit at my handwork through the harem visit, archaically
smiling at intervals, making small-talk with some kind of house-friend.
She's got him facing her now, his back is somnolent,
heavy with uncritical contempt. From getting no depths,
she's progressed to getting no sense. His mind slowly sorts
tools, weapons, cordage, decking, bartered for in foreign places.
Her hand on his shoulder, she's thrashing about reliving
(blonde hair cleaving and parting) her divine self,
her daringly innocent prime. He's past seeing it.

Ithaca has nothing like it. Of course we pleaded harem
against the nuisance of molesters. But now with my son in charge
women of rank as well as peasant women
go about free-striding, frank in talk and enticement.

I sit with crochet, as long since, keeping an eye on it,
seeing it through. Unexceptionable. Till in the minutes
of absence and opposition, his turned back and unmoving head
blank as sea-swilled crags to her rudderless veering
— from her wheedling to her argumentative —
I sense the depth of rock, wind-fed with privateers,
that I shall never speak of, and he half-forgets;
those years of shores, send-up of the long-resolved landfall,
the crews and peoples, quaysides and stranger hearth-welcomes
where sacred above droves of men he embraces, most honoured,
the ancient royal witch of her bitter island —
beast-attended Circe bronze-eyed, with strong ankles,
his one-time Aeaean woman.

## BORGES AT 73

Bone. No finality, but a frame.
The nose drawn up towards bone.
Hand, pen, tongue retreating
into bone. Into the depots of Borges.

Before bone, coral. Reefs, tempting sea-level.
And peopled, in myriads, on principles
to be approached by induction. Look!
they are out in the pool behind you, green on red.
And up, two pools ahead. Only here,
with your sandshoes wet through, scuffing the lapping
wash in the island's lee, coral looks one substance,
uninhabited.

Be still. Examine narrowly, without stooping or speaking.
O richly-caparisoned polypi!
insatiable vortices, treasury of sensors!
utterers of intolerable mathematics!

Their eyes enlarge fragile caverns.
With their corrosive unidentifiable
jelly that is metal that is flesh,
they abolish not-seeing.

In Borges' skull of an assymetrical lemon,
an urchin labours this terminal course
of convolutions. Until (if ever) the catch flicks,
to set at large the implied time-bomb's
seedless interior.

Borges is drying out like a drowned volume,
so many select libraries written
in its margins and over its end-leaves,
and metaphysically crossed with the printed text
which is both previous and simultaneous.

So many libraries unwritten
stock the mere odour of its binding
partly surviving sea-water's
necessary passage.

From his submarine institute,
precisely oriented to oceanic rages
amid its eminence of reef,
Borges is about to transmit
deciphered portions of arcane
memorabilia:

(The transmissions are curious but brief, and there is always
the question of the identity of the sender. Constantly they
touch on the twin opposites, alike impossible, of a concept
never foreshadowed in the history of thought, and of anni-
hilation.

   This message appears to come from a different trans-
mitter. The source has been traced to a similar pre-oceanic
depth where, at the top of the darkening slope of con-
tinental shelf, the debris of light's forcing-ground — the relics
of habitation — yield to the abyss.)

   In the reception-room of the poet and architect Shashu
   Hsin-Feng, mother of twin philosopher-princes and
   seventh Empress of the incestuous blood-royal of Outer
   Chu-Shu'an a century before it was dragged at the
   hooves of Ghengis Khan's stallions, she caused to be
   sunk into the pavement an extraordinary elliptical
   stone basin. In the waters of this pool she satisfied her
   curious taste for bestiality with turtles — those living
   topographies, that figure our shield-shaped skies turned
   away from us, interacting in dark complicity with a
   soft underside of Earth. The scene of her copulations
   was completely lined with a mosaic so richly devised,
   so skilfully contrived of silver, coloured stones and
   precious gems, many of which no longer have a name in

any language spoken today, that much-travelled connoisseurs have not scrupled to call it the most perfectly intricate in the world.

Nightly Borges removes from it one tiny tessera, each time a different one.

Without fail, the gap reveals a further pattern, so marvellous that it makes the first mosaic (with that tessera removed), although the germ of the second-discovered one, and its primary disseminator to men, a mere indistinguishable fragment of a motif in the new, huge and probably infinite design beyond; unless indeed the removal of one of its tesserae should permit a glimpse of yet more majestic and complicated perspectives. This last is a feat Borges has constantly in mind, but will never know whether he has at last actually performed.

Through the gap of one tessera, the waters purified by virgin priests for the notorious impieties of a degenerate woman drain, leaving not one drop; Borges' constant removal of the tessera is the means whereby the universal symmetry is nightly bathed in the liquor of the Empress's pleasures. Whether the Empress Shashu Hsin-Feng knew of his visits is not recorded in the surviving five books of her reflections on history, found inscribed on turtle-shell, still less in the popular saying on love which tradition has ascribed to her, and which is all that remains of her atrocious carnality.

**PARENTHESIS:**

*for David Albenda*

the Adirondacks, last week of the season;
blue air pausing, car windows sink at wish,
tree patterns weave in water, time for the gleam
of scissors on rock, laid open by flight and ready there
unrusted, seventeen feet down in brown lake water.
Later, warmer and nearer, at a step, at a dip
minnows and their dark-dart twins browsing in mud-shallows
— a finger, a shoe-tip — they shake like filings to a magnet,
governed. The wandering-lilied bay sighs,
that was not its way, and resumes them to lake courses.
But summer weekenders are reaching for wallets and bags,
all cars turn east and south. Ice moves nearer
as the race of lake-men start to the change of season.
The corpse under the cliff-wall mumbles her tale
of tied arms and flesh detained and eight-foot hair
fed on a cleft of the lake-bed thirty years,
who would now be an old woman. Whose college made out
on a query, a fiction, whose students never fathomed
her stirrings, a grotesque mermaid given to brown
wintering of wars and a billion more punctual lives;
who was slime at a breath, her water-miracle surrendered.

I wonder about water-lives. I question the face
that waited half-young while those who had known it young
met it in musings of old age. I swim the parasite
hair-wave lengthening into legend, I try if a slab
of water keeps off memory or holds down longing.
Out of timeless three hundred feet you expect a death,
the remainder. The end to air and earth questions,
the body found, the one-time lover met.
Drag all you will, the water-woman grows
monstrously sinuous amid her monstrous tide
of clues threaded with all the pawnshop past.

Water - life (1) 5/20                    26/75

What sort of life she's wanting, who can tell?
but she's persistent. What to want of her —
there she drowned, and everything they dredge up
to settle by the way of air and earth piety
has never left the water. The hair still feeds.

Time to move on, to bless the innocent water
and blueberry pie pavilions of holiday air.
Wave to old Whiteface, whose big toe nudging lake-caverns
quivers no distrust to his sky-thought head,
his ice-scored rock-fall sides. Drop the clover tassels,
pick up the shoes and go; to ride exclaiming
in the last boat-load of the afternoon
the summer-fallen rapids of a river chasm
and cross the plains, to dine in Montreal.

Delivered, with log-blunt paws of a troll-faced boatman
gouging his pine-green region for anecdotes,
more than you looked to show me at Lake Placid:
parenthesis.